Make a Gingerbread Man

Conni Medina

Conni Medina

Consultant

Timothy Rasinski, Ph.D.
Kent State University

Publishing Credits

Dona Herweck Rice, *Editor-in-Chief*

Lee Aucoin, *Creative Director*

Conni Medina, M.A.Ed., *Editorial Director*

Jamey Acosta, *Editor*

Robin Erickson, *Designer*

Stephanie Reid, *Photo Editor*

Rachelle Cracchiolo, M.S.Ed., *Publisher*

Image Credits
Cover Jason Pappo; p.3 Ruth Black/Dreamstime.com; p.4 Monkey Business Images/ Shutterstock; p.5 Jason Pappo; p.6 Quang Ho/Shutterstock, Eric Boucher/Shutterstock, Sean MacD/ Shutterstock; p.7 kyoshino/iStockphoto, VVO/Shutterstock, Brooke Fuller/Shutterstock; p.8 James Skelton/Shutterstock; pp.9–11 Jason Pappo; p.12 Stephanie Reid; pp. 13–18 Jason Pappo

Based on writing from *TIME For Kids.*

TIME For Kids and the *TIME For Kids* logo are registered trademarks of TIME Inc. Used under license.

Teacher Created Materials

5301 Oceanus Drive
Huntington Beach, CA 92649-1030
http://www.tcmpub.com

ISBN 978-1-4333-3594-5

Ding! The timer sounds.
Out of the oven come hot,
fresh gingerbread cookies.

Gingerbread cookies are often made during winter. These spicy cookies are a tasty treat on a cold day.

You can make a craft that looks like a gingerbread man.

Before you start, get
the things you need.
You need a **paper bag**,
scissors, and a **marker**.

You need **ribbon**, **colored paper**, and glue, too.

Start with a paper bag.
Turn it facedown.

Use a marker to draw
the shape of a gingerbread
man.

Use the scissors to cut out
the shape you just drew.

Now you've made the
body of a gingerbread man.

Cut a piece of ribbon. It should be twice as long as the gingerbread man.

Fold the ribbon to make a loop. Tape the ends of the ribbon to the back of the gingerbread man.

Now it's time to make
your gingerbread man
special!

Cut out pieces of colored
paper to make eyes, a nose,
and a mouth. Glue them on.

To finish, add buttons
and a scarf.

Use the colored paper to
make the shapes you need.
Glue them on.

Share your gingerbread
man with someone special.

Glossary

colored paper

ribbon

marker

scissors

paper bag

Words to Know

buttons	scarf
colored paper	share
craft	sounds
ding	special
gingerbread	timer
ribbon	